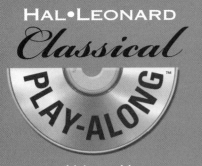

HAL•LEONARD
Classical PLAY-ALONG™

Volume 11

T0078946

Giovanni Battista
PERGOLESI
(1710-1736)

Flute Concerto in G Major

The Hal Leonard Classical Play-Along™ series allows you to work through great classical works systematically and at any tempo with accompaniment.

Tracks 2-4 on the CD demonstrate the concert version of each movement. After tuning your instrument to Track 1 you can begin practicing the piece. Using the Amazing Slow-Downer technology included on the CD, you can adjust the recording to any tempo you like without altering the pitch. (Note that when using Amazing Slow-Downer, the CD will stop after each track instead of playing continuously.) The full cadenzas are played only in the concert version.

- Track No. $\boxed{1}$ – tuning notes
- Track numbers in circles $\bigcirc$ – concert version
- Track numbers in diamonds ◆ – play-along version

CONCERT VERSION

Guilio Giannelli Viscardi, Flute

Russian Philharmonic Orchestra Moscow

Konstantin Krimets, Conductor

ISBN 978-1-4234-6250-7

HAL•LEONARD®
CORPORATION

7777 W. BLUEMOUND RD. P.O.BOX 13819 MILWAUKEE, WI 53213

In Australia Contact:
Hal Leonard Australia Pty. Ltd.
4 Lentara Court
Cheltenham, Victoria, 3192 Australia
Email: ausadmin@halleonard.com.au

Visit Hal Leonard Online at
www.halleonard.com

CONCERTO

for Flute in G Major

I ②

G. B. Pergolesi (1710 - 1736)